Anne Reeve Aldrich

The Rose of Flame

And Other Poems of Love

Anne Reeve Aldrich

The Rose of Flame
And Other Poems of Love

ISBN/EAN: 9783744694957

Printed in Europe, USA, Canada, Australia, Japan

Cover: Foto ©Thomas Meinert / pixelio.de

More available books at **www.hansebooks.com**

THE ROSE OF FLAME

AND OTHER POEMS OF LOVE

BY

ANNE REEVE ALDRICH

"And for one moment mine eyes were unsealed, and I beheld both Heaven and Hell. And I shrank back with a great awe, and asked: 'What wouldst thou teach me?' And the Master replied: 'Thou hast seen Love.'"

NEW YORK AND LONDON

G. P. PUTNAM'S SONS

The Knickerbocker Press

1889

Press of
G. P. Putnam's Sons
New York

CONTENTS.

A WORD BEFORE THESE VERSES.

To ——— ———.

These from me to you.   No song worth singing
Came until I stood within your shadow,
—Felt the stinging tears within mine eyelids,
—Learned some songs are born with heart's upheaval,
Tears of blood, and all the pangs of travail.

These across the snow-clad miles I send you.
Would, instead, I felt your breath upon me,
Would, instead, my trembling lips could murmur
In your ear, three words, that in their compass
Hold the music of all poets' singing !

THE ROSE OF FLAME.

NEW EDEN.

In that first Eden, Love gave birth to Shame,
  And died of horror at its loathsome child.
Let us slay Shame, and bury it to-day,—
  Yea, hide it in this second Eden's wild,
This dim, strange place, where, for aught we two
      know,
No man hath stepped since God first made it so.

Now, dream we are alone in all the earth.
  Say wouldst thou weep if all save we were dead?
I would not weep, but closer to my breast
  Would press the golden glories of thy head,
Rejoicing that none other of my race
Should feed his eyes upon thy wondrous face.

Look at this tangled snare of undergrowth,
   These low-branched trees that darken all below ;
Drink in the hot scent of this noontide air,
   And hear, far off, some distant river flow,
Lamenting ever till it finds the sea.
New Life, new World, what 's Shame to thee and
    me ?

Let us slay Shame ; we shall forget his grave
   Locked in the rapture of our lone embrace.
Yet what if there should rise, as once of old,
   New wonder of this new, yet ancient place :
An angel, with a whirling sword of flame,
To drive us forth forever in God's name !

A WANDERER.

THE snows lie thick around his door,
  —That door made fast by bar and lock.
He will not heed thee, trembling, chilled ;
  He will not hear thy piteous knock.
Poor wandering Heart, canst thou not see
There is no welcome here for thee ?

The air is numb with frost and night.
  O wait no longer in the snow,
For lo, from yonder latticed pane
  Faint music and the fire-light's glow ;
He hath another guest in state,
And thou, poor Heart, thou art too late !

LOVE'S CHANGE.

I WENT to dig a grave for Love,
But the earth was so stiff and cold,
That though I strove through the bitter night,
I could not break the mold.

And I said : " Must he lie in my house in state,
And stay in his wonted place?
Must I have him with me another day,
With that awful change in his face?"

LENT.

Aн, the road is a weary road
That leads one on to God,
And all too swift the eager race
To suit a lagging pace,
And far, far distant looks the goal
To the most patient soul.
So I forsook the sharp set road,
And walked where pleasant herbs were sowed.
I flung the sandals from tired feet,
And strayed where honeyed flowers grew sweet,
Nor strained tense nerves, nor onward pressed,
But made the goal his breast.
His circling arms my Heaven I made,
And, save to him, no more I prayed.
So for my sin I paid the price
Of endless joys of Paradise.

THE ROSE OF FLAME.

Good fellow-pilgrims, go your way.
For me 't is all in vain to pray.
I weep, when o'er the windy track
Your victors' hymns float echoing back,
But still I know, with eyelids wet,
I could return, but not forget.

DREAMS.

So still I lay within his arms
   He dreamed I was asleep,
Across my lips I felt his breath
   Like burning breezes creep.
I felt his watchful, searching gaze
   Though closed eyes cannot see ;
I felt his warm and tender grasp
   More closely prison me.

The waking dream was all too sweet
   For me to wish to sleep.
I was too far beyond Earth's woes
   To speak, or smile, or weep.
How after this, could I endure
   The troublous times of Age and Tears,
To sit and wait for Death to dawn
   Across the midnight of my years !

Love will not stay, though we entreat ;
  Death will not come at call.
Ah, to return to life and grief !
  Ah, having risen to fall !
I felt his mouth burn on my own ;
  I raised my eyes to his eyes' deep.
He thought his kiss had wakened me,
  —He dreamed I was asleep !

TWO SONGS.

I.

OUT of the burning East,
  And over three blue seas,
He came to melt my icy pride,
  And storm my heart's hushed ease.

O few are found to mend,
  But many mad to mar.
Were mens' hearts here not cruel enough
  That thou needst come so far?

*   *   *   *   *   *

II.

How can I from my past go free?
You laid its fetters' weight on me;
You locked them, and have lost the key.

And I have worn them in all lands;
Nor will they drop from my dead hands,
But rust on through the thick grave-bands.

AN AWAKENING.

Love had forgotten and gone to sleep ;
   Love had forgotten the present and past.
I was so glad when he ceased to weep,
   " Now he is quiet," I whispered, " at last."

What sent you here on that night of all nights,
   Breaking his slumber, dreamless and deep ?
—Just as I whispered below my breath :
   " Love has forgotten and gone to sleep." '

THE LAST MOMENT.

So, all is said, and all is done.
No more for me this side o' the sun.
Who knows ?   I may wake in pleasant weather,
Where later we two may walk,—together.
Who knows ?   The old love may rise in him,
And his eyes be wet when mine own are dim,
And well it may end that was well begun ;
But it will not be this side o' the sun.

Ah, but the days here on earth go fast ;
He will remember, and come at last.
O what shall I care for Paradise
While I watch for him there, with eager eyes ?
He has forgotten ; but soon or late
He will remember, and I can wait.
When the tide turns, it swells full fast ;
He will remember, and come at last.

UNDER THE ROSE.

HE moved with trembling fingers
  From my throat, the band of red,
And a band of burning kisses
  His lips set there instead.

Then he tied again the ribbon.
  "I will hide them, Love," said he,
"And the secret of thy necklace
  None shall know, save thee and me."

It was just a foolish fancy,
  But from that day to this,
I wore the crimson ribbon
  To hide my lover's kiss.

He has gone, and love is over,
  But this blade within my hand,
Still shall hide our secret kisses
  With another crimson band.

14

IMMOLATION.

Take her, and lay her head upon thy breast,
   And be thou blest beyond thy heart's desire ;
And as the star that ushers in the dawn
   Fades from the sight in morning's glow and
      fire,
So, having heralded thy break of day,
'T is Nature's law that I no longer stay.

A path was I that led thee to thy goal ;
   Forget the path, since now the goal is won.
That was its proper place in all the land,
   And it was made to set thy feet upon.
Its blessing is that all its course did tend
To bring thee to thy journey's happy end.

THE END.

Do you recall that little room
   Close blinded from the searching sun,
So dim, my blossoms dreamed of dusk?
   And shut their petals one by one.
—And then a certain crimson eve,
   The death of day upon the tide ;
How all its blood spread on the waves,
   And stained the waters far and wide.
         Ah, you forget ;
         But I remember yet.

When I awake in middle night,
   And stretch warm hands to touch your face,
There is no chance that I shall find
   Aught but your chill and empty place.
I have no bitter word to say,
   The Past is worth this anguish sore,
—But mouth to mouth, and heart to heart,
   No more on earth, O God, no more !
         For Love is dead ;
         Would 't were I, instead.

ARCADIA.

Sunlight on us, Love ;
Not a shadow comes between.
  Midway of the field we stand,
  Heart in heart and hand in hand :
And all the land is green.

Look around thee, Love,—
Naught but meadows shining fair,
  Save, as far as eye can see,
  Long, low hills, clothed tenderly
By the veils of mist they wear.

But below us, Love,
Hidden by the meadow's rise,
  Whispers brokenly a stream
  Like a voice heard in a dream ;
Clear its current as thine eyes.

17

Thou must linger, Love,
For a little on this side ;
    Both its banks are soft with moss.
    Grieve not, Dear, that I shall cross,
For but shallow is its tide.

Canst not see it, Love ?
Nay, Heart's Dearest, nor can I ;
    But in pauses to mine ear
    Comes the sound thou canst not hear,
Filling silence with a sigh.

Smile again, dear Love,
Brighter day was never seen.
    Pull these blossoms for thy hair ;
    Spring-time's joy is in the air,
And all the land is green.

LOVE, THE DESTROYER.

Love is a Fire;
Nor Shame, nor Pride can well withstand Desire.
"For what are they," we cry, "that they should dare
To keep, O Love, the haughty look they wear?
Nay, burn the victims, O thou sacred Fire,
That with their death thou mayst but flame the higher.
Let them feel once the fierceness of thy breath,
And make thee still more beauteous with their death."

Love is a Fire;
But ah, how short-lived is the flame Desire!
Love, having burnt whatever once we cherished,
And blackened all things else, itself hath perished.
And now alone in gathering night we stand,
Ashes and ruin stretch on either hand.
Yet while we mourn, our sad hearts whisper low:
"We served the mightiest God that man can know."

TWO PARTINGS.

HE said good-bye with laughing eyes,
Too careless of me to be wise
  And see I grieved, since he must go.
With weary tears, through night and day,
In thought, I follow on his way,
For he must go, and I must stay.
    ——I dread the bitter winds that blow.

Now time, at last, brings near a day
When I must go, and he must stay,
  And I, like him, shall smile to go.
And when he says good-bye to me,
Although he weep, I shall not see,
But if in thoughts he follow me,
    ——He need not dread the winds that blow.

THE PILGRIM.

THERE stood a pilgrim at the palace gate,
  Who fain would enter at the Court of Love,
And knocking, as he turned, and stood to wait,
  About him circled many a crested dove.
Sweating he stood beneath the August noon,
And white with dust his cloak and travelling shoon.

And as at last it opened to his knock,
  Within there gaped a goodly company.
Who looked upon him with a curious gaze,
  As if his state and quest they fain would see.
And " Step thou close," said one, " and tell us all
What thou dost seek here at Love's entrance hall."

The throng seemed weary with some weight of woe,
  And part wore ruined garlands on the head,
And some, all naked in the summer heat
  With grievous stripes were furrowed black, or red.
But bruised or weary, each one on his face
  Wore the same look of mingled grief and grace.

" I come, "—the pilgrim said, and half abashed
   Gazed on the small sere grasses at his feet,—
" To enter in the service of King Love,
   Whose bitterest dole, they say, is passing sweet.
Him would I serve, with body and with soul,
And yield me utterly to his control."

He spoke, and lo, looks swift as fluttering birds
   Flew back and forth from those who gazed on him.
And one young maid drew close and touched his
      arm,
   And with compassionate eyes grown wet and
      dim,
And swelling throat, and tender voice, she said ;
" Our King gives golden moments ; hours of lead.

" Our King's unequal wage to those who serve,
   We know, yet serve him meekly none the less,
And if to-night He smite thee with sore stripes,
   To-morrow He may look on thee and bless,
And by that look, be thy wounds ne'er so sore,
They will be healed, and anguish thee no more.

" Thou must yield up thy soul into His hand,
   Even as thy body to His governing.
Thy thoughts are His ; thy lips are also His,
   And praises of none other shalt thou sing.
He is a jealous Lord to serve withal,
And dread His vengeance, if thou slip or fall.

" His armor thou must wear ; 't will weigh thee
     down,
   And by it all thy body shall be torn.
And weary watches thou perforce must keep,
   Nor think to sleep till breaking of the morn.
But laboring patient for a weary space,
Perchance he deigns to show to thee His face."

The pilgrim listened, leaning by the wall,
   And absently wrote figures with his staff.
And then at last he raised his glowing face,
   And in his throat they heard a hard, glad laugh.
" And is *that* all? And some day, may I hope
The while I toil, and serving blindly, grope

" For ways that best shall please my Lord and King,
   That ere I die, He once may look on me ?—
That I for one rich moment of my life
   May gaze, half-dazzled on His majesty ?
Enough, enough, that possible great bliss
Is worth a dozen lives as cramped as this."

And then they pressed around him, man and maid,
   And in his mouth he felt a kiss of flame.
" Now cast from thee the sandals of vain pride,"
   They said, " and throw thou off the robe of
     shame.
They will but cumber thee by day and night,
Beside, no man may enter, thus bedight."

And then the gate swung closed upon its hinge,
   And as the novice entered with the throng,
Upon the silence of the scorching noon
   Wavered most faintly back a chorused song,
Solemn as death, and sweet as an embrace,
For they who sang had looked upon Love's face.

ROSE SONG.

PLANT, above my lifeless heart
   Crimson roses, red as blood.
As if the love, pent there so long
   Were pouring forth its flood.

Then, through them, my heart may tell,
   Its Past of Love and Grief,
And I shall feel them grow from it,
   And know a vague relief.

Through rotting shroud shall feel their roots,
   And unto them myself shall grow,
And when I blossom at her feet,
   She, on that day, shall know !

NOCTURNE.

THE moon has gone to sleep,
   It is dark here under the trees,
There is presage of storm in the hot, hushed air
   And never a stir of breeze.

I lie here spent on his breast,
   All the war in my soul is dead,
I have struggled, and I am conquered at last,
   No more strife, let me rest instead.

What so good in life or death,
   As to feel his warm breath on my face,
To be thrown here, storm-tossed against his breast,
   My shelter and hiding-place.

O the hush of the Summer night,
   O the Silence that wraps us round,
O the Silence of vanquished and conqueror,
   Unbroken by stir or sound.

O why, through the rapture and rest,
   Must run this one pain like a snake—
Only an hour at the best for this dream,
   And blankness and chill when you wake.

Crying and wailing at light,
   Soon will this night-hush be gone,
Swiftly these dark hours are flying by,
   Then the agony of the dawn !

IN SHADOW.

YES, go ; the night is changing as we wait,
   Black clouds stretch fingers out and clutch the
      moon,
   The mists hang low ; the winds begin to croon,
Filling the air with wailings desolate.

Some night, with lips too cold to shape a cry,
   I shall remember : " We stood hand in hand,
   Dull moonlight on a sodden stretch of land,
Low-hanging vapor, and the winds' half sigh."

A NEW YEAR.

THY bride is waiting in the kirk,
The wedding wine waits in thy hall.
        Adieu.
For me, the stream's cold tide to drink,
Where once we lingered at its brink,
The kirk-yard waits thy Summer's work.
        Adieu.

For her, the sweetest flowers that grow,
For me, the faded Autumn grass,
        Adieu.
For me, the dead leaves' tarnished gold.
Ah, linger not, for once of old,
Love, thou did'st stay when I said "Go!"
        Adieu.

For her, the pearl wrought marriage-dress,
The choir, the Mass, the ring of gold.
   Adieu.
For me, the chants that night-birds sing.
My hand in thine, I asked no ring,
Nor blessed by love, the Church to bless.
   Adieu.

For her, the wedding sheets are spread,
For her, the cup of Love and Life.
   Adieu.
For me, the cup of Love and Death.
Then earth to earth, as the priest saith,
My bed of love, and my last bed.
   Adieu.

PRESCIENCE.

SIGHED a wave in middle ocean,
   "O to reach the warm, white shore !
On its breast to lie in silence,
   Hushed in peace, forevermore.

"Ah, I know what lies before me,
   I, at last, shall clasp the shore.
Break my heart on it one moment,
   Then moan on, forevermore."

IN EXTREMIS.

THE sacred tapers flickered fair,
The priest has gone with Host and prayer ;
I heard the " Nunc Dimittis " said,
—Not with the heart, but with the head.

Though I, the while, lay dying near,
This was all my heart could hear :
" I love thee, lay thy lips on mine,
Thy kisses turn my head like wine."

And this was all my heart could see,
Instead of the cross held out to me,
That well-known small and scented room,
Made sweetly dusk by curtain's gloom.

And this was all my heart could feel,
Spite of these pains like stabbing steel,
The throbbing pulses of thy breast,
Where, weary, I was wont to rest.

O what shall come to me, alas !
Whose soul so soon in death must pass
The soul too wholly thine to dwell
On hope of heaven, or dread of hell.

If heaven, that awful glassy sea,
May still reflect some memory.
If hell, not all eternal fire,
Can quite burn out the old desire.

Instead of name of pitying saint
Breathed as the passing soul's last plaint,
Thy name will be my latest breath.
Who wast my life, who art my death.

FIVE SHORT SONGS.

I.

AN ANNIVERSARY.

My languor grieves you, and my restless sigh ?
Is there no wish your love can gratify ?
Yes, journey till you find, and bring me here
The one who kissed me close this day last year !

II.

AN ENCHANTRESS.

I can vouch no more for the Future
  Than I can for the morrow's fair weather,
And my Past is well seamed with by-paths ;
  We can scarcely retrace them together.

And why should my Past give you trouble,
  If its secrets it never discloses ?
Why to-night should you grasp at the Future ?
  You have me, and the moonlight and roses !

III.

SERVITUDE.

The church was dim at vespers.
　My eyes were on the Rood.
But yet I felt thee near me,
　In every drop of blood.

In helpless, trembling bondage
　My soul's weight lies on thee,
O call me not at dead of night,
　Lest I should come to thee !

IV.

A FÊTE-DAY.

They brought me snowy roses,
　A picture of my Saint,
A little dove, whose tender note
　Was like a virgin's plaint.
But you ?　You brought fierce kisses
　That caught my heart in snare,
They crushed the snowy roses,
　That decked my throat and hair.

The pictured Saint, in anguish,
   Gazed down from carven frame,
. And prayed, perhaps in heaven,
   For her who bears her name.
The frightened dove moaned softly,
   With ruffled wing and crest.
And never since will nestle
   As once, within my breast !

V.

LIFE.

Far where the snow whitens the marshy sod,
Lives one who nightly speaks my name to God,
With simple faith, its saintliness shall bear
An added weight with Heaven to grant his prayer.
And in a city church-yard, calm at last,
Lies one who cursed me as his sad soul passed.
"God pity me !" he cried, "This is my shame,
That e'en to curse thee, I should speak thy name !"
Which gauged me best ?   Ah, friend, I cannot say.
To know myself, I wait till Judgment Day.

IN EXCULPATION.

You seared both eyes with kisses,
    And then bade me, blinded, go.
Nor leave betraying foot-prints
    Upon your life's pure snow.

Ah, Love, you should remember
    Ere you set blind captives free
They cannot find the by-paths
    Who can no longer see !

Ah, Love, 't was your cruel folly
    That set me journeying so,
And hoped to find, thereafter,
    No foot-prints on the snow.

THE ROSE OF FLAME.

GOD-like ignorance have they
   Who the voyage dare undertake.
Yet men venture every day
   For the mystic Blossom's sake.
Smile and weep for such as they,
If perchance ye know the way.
Smile for foe, and weep for friend,
Strange the journey, sure its end.

Through wide, twilight seas the course.
   He may start from any port.
Fate alone stands at the helm,
   Be the sailing long or short.
Night or day or weary week,
Still she guides, and does not speak.
No wild gale, or tempest's wrath
Dares to cross his vessel's path.

And what place of dreams is this,
 Where the keel slides in the sand?
Never mortal's eyes but once
 Gaze on such a magic strand.
The shore is veiled by mists of Shame
Where grows the luring Rose of Flame.
Bare sand, without a shrub or tree,
And vapor white, and whispering sea.

And now Fate holds him by the hand,
 And leads him inland, till no more
The mist of Shame cleaves to the sand,
 And distant grows the sea and shore.
Out of the desert, stretching bare,
Come dizzy scents that load the air.
Blindly and unfatigued he goes ;
He breathes the perfume of the Rose.

Nearer—he feels the burning heat.
 Can desert hold a flower like this ?
He sees, is blinded by its glow ;
 The scent is like a clinging kiss.

The perfume deepens to a pang,
And in his brain strange music sang,
Such as lost Spirits sing in Hell.
Then,—days,—or years ; he best can tell.

Withered, sere, and scorched at heart,
   He must seek the world once more.
Never shall he sail again
   Through such seas, to touch such shore,
And the memory of that strand
Makes him loathe all other land,
And no flower seems worth the name,
Since he saw the Rose of Flame.

A MARCH SONG.

My love stands in the falling snow,
  She will not hear me woo,
Rest, little flakes, upon her breast,
  'T is colder far than you.

Yet spite of wintry wind, she wears
  A knot of violets blue.
Die, little flowers, upon her breast
  And would that I were you.

A RETURN TO THE VALLEY.

BEHOLD me at thy feet. Alone I climbed
  And wandered through the mountain land of Art
Amid God's awful snows; the keen thin air
  Pierced through my brain, and chilled me at the
    heart.

Behold me at thy feet. A famished heart
  Does ill to travel by such paths as these.
Better for me to seek this vale once more,
  Better for me to crouch here at thy knees.

Behold me at thy feet. And thou dost stretch
  No tender hand to raise me to thy breast.
Ah, 't is a foolish bird that hopes to find
  Untouched, in leafless hedge, its last year's nest.

I will depart, and seek again the heights,
  Above hot love, or wholesome hate of foes.
But from this day my pilgrim feet must leave
  A track of blood across the awful snows.

A PLEA.

Yes, thy love was passing sweet,
Still, thy gift is incomplete.
Round it to its perfect sphere,
Ere thou kiss, and leave me, Dear.
Lest in future—who can say?
I should curse thee for this day.
I would not outlive to-night,
Let me die, while love 's at height.
Life has nothing left to prove,
Give me death, as well as love!

SISTER SAINT MAGDALEN.

I MET you in the street to-day,
    In sombre robe, and cloak, and wimple.
The folds of white around your chin,
    Strove all in vain to hide its dimple.

You held a basket in the hand
    That once clasped mine in stress of passion.
A small child from your parish school,
    Tramped by your side in stolid fashion.

Strange World! I little dreamed that you
    For one sweet hour of love and folly,
Must cleanse your soul by penances,
    And dreary nights of melancholy.

I wonder if, in your chill cell,
    The lips that kissed mine never falter,
And through the solemn hours repeat
    The hymns, and rosary, and psalter.

In vain I asked your eyes to-day ;
　　As quick as thought you dropped your lashes.
Perhaps 't was fancy made me dream
　　That fire still slept beneath the ashes.

Ah well, the night grows cold, my pipe
　　Is almost out.　I wonder, wonder
What memories haunt your heart to-night,
　　What convent roof you 're sheltering under.

If in your prayers my graceless name
　　Is whispered in the silence nightly,
'T is man's return for too much love
　　To hold the heaped up measure lightly.

'T is—God knows what it is, but I,
　　Who with a smile such lot assigned you,
Would scale your convent wall to-night,
　　And kiss and kill you, could I find you !

IN NOVEMBER.

BROWN earth-line meets gray heaven,
  And all the land looks sad,
But Love's the little leaven
  That works the whole world glad.
Sigh, bitter wind, lower, frore clouds of gray,
My Love and I are living now in May !

COLOR SONG.

WHITE and red, wine and bread,
We ate and drank, our wooing sped.
Alas, the measure of secret pleasure,
My mother's curse is on my head.

Green and blue, land and sea,
Over them both you fled from me.
Ah mad, sweet wooing, 't was my undoing,
No more on Earth your face I see.

A MESSAGE TO MY DEAR.

Ah my love, I am with you heart and soul,
   Heart and soul in spite of them all,
Spite of Dame Reason, who keeps me here,
   Spite of Dame Conscience with iron thrall.

Only the body, that throbs and pants,
   Cannot get free from their binding chain.
It must pine here, whether it will or no,
   Never to thrill in thy arms again.

But my Heart, she speaks to the cold, stern shrews :
   " Guard thou the body, but I am free,
Keep what thou canst, but know, good dames,
   Mine is the joy of memory.

" Mine are a thousand raptures past,
   Passionate noontides and moonlit nights,
Keep thou the body, good dames, an' thou canst
   But know that the heart takes its swallow flights ! "

A FALLEN BLOSSOM.

THERE 's not a star in the sky,
  The air hangs thick with mist,
And the rain is wet on the throat he praised,
  And chill on the lips he kissed.

Ah, well for that summer day,
With its loitering breeze from the south ;
But alas for the winter, no word for me,
  No kiss for the poor changed mouth.

Ah, well for the Summer Rose
  With its beauty undashed by a tear.
But alas for the Rose in the Autumn rains,
  And alas for the sad New Year !

And if his tears should fall
  Where he kissed again and again,
Ah, God ! would it be too late to know
  A tear from a drop of this rain—
  If 't were too late to know pain ?

THE PORTRAIT.

LET others drape the face
They dare no more to see, in shrouding fold,
And teach themselves, in all the gloom and cold
Of coming winter, that there lies no spark
In the hid eyes, to warm and light their dark,
 Nor look again upon its blinded grace.

Thou canst be seen,
O thou beloved Face, by all who care to gaze.
From me alone, bright sun of my dead days,
A veil of tears forever hides thy light,
But dawn of Heaven shall break on earthly night,
 And God shall rend the veil that lies between !

WHEN I WAS THINE.

"Ricordati da me quand 'ero teco."—Tuscan Rispetto.

THE sullen rain breaks on the convent window,
  The distant chanting dies upon mine ears.
—Soon comes the morn for which my soul hath
      languished,
  For which my soul hath yearned these many
      years ;
Forget of me this life which I resign,
Think of me in the days when I was thine.

Forget the paths my weary feet have travelled,
  The thorns and stones that pierced them as I
      went ;
These later days of prayer and scourge and pen-
      ance,
  These hours of anguish now so nearly spent.
Forget I left thy life for life divine,
Think of me in the days when I was thine.

Forget the rigid brow as thou wilt see it,
  The folded eyelids, and the quiet mouth.
Think how my eyes grew brighter at thy coming,
  Think of those fervid noontides in the South.
Think when my kisses made life half divine,
Think of me in the days when I was thine.

Forget this nearer past, I do adjure thee,
  Remember only what was long ago.
Think when our love was fire unquenched by
    ashes,
  Think of our Spring, and not this Winter's snow.
Forget me as I lie, past speech or sign.
Think of me in the days when I was thine.

PREMONITIONS.

I.

Here I kneel in the Church, and the Altar Throne,
    dim in the twilight,
Shows sundry points a-gleam, by the swinging red
    lamp of the Presence.
It is so cold, on the rail here, before me, my tears
    lie in ice-drops.
Cold as a stone, too, the hand that has beaten my
    breast in my praying.
Haunted again, even here, in this Church's gray,
    frozen silence.
Mixed with my prayers and my tears, the Past that
    has led to the Future.
Feet, that have strayed here to-night, ye have a
    path yet to travel,
Shaped for you, destined for you, but its ending
    lies veiled in the shadows.
Only a part I can see, far enough to set you a-
    journey,

Not as a dream of the night, or a heated midsum-
mer fancy,

This is the certain foreknowledge, that thus I must
do, it is fated.

II.

Over wide miles in the dusk, with a soul full of
calmness and silence,

Only fulfilling my life's plain logical end in com-
pleteness.

Then through the streets all astir with lights and
the sounds of late traffic,

Then a corridor, noisy, and full of echoing voices.

Then a wide flight of stairs, that await my unhast-
ing footsteps,

Stairs, that ere they were built, were ordained I
should traverse, ascending,

Stairs to which all my journeys by land and by
ocean have led me.

These I shall climb, soon or late, and the time is, I
think, drawing nearer.

Only a threshold to cross, and then face to face
with what shall be.

III.

" Take me, or leave me, I come. I am yours as to
flesh and to spirit.

Fashion the soul, as you will, and doom it to Hell
or to Heaven.

And of the body, 't is yours, and humble to spurn-
ing or worship."

World, what of you ? If 't is well, and he crush
me at this to his bosom,

Never a word of dispraise in that ultimate rapture
can reach me.

Who, for their mortal delight, would take in its
lieu your approval ?

And, if instead, a cold glance from him should
pierce me at heart's core,

Scarcely, I think, I shall heed your comment of
scorn on the morrow,

For by that morrow my ears will be filled with
brown, hurrying ripples

Of that small muddy river, that winds round the
edge of the city.

SMILES AND TEARS.

MINE eyes have looked upon the earth
Through such strange years since God first bade
    them wake !
And first they smiled to find it all so fair,
So much to be beloved for beauty's sake.
And then they wept, to find the earth so sad,
To know the worm lay hid in beauty's core.
And since that day they have forgot to smile,
And only have known tears forevermore.
But when God bids them wake that second day,
They shall forget to weep, and smile alway.

A BALLAD OF THE BELL.

THE bell hangs still in the belfry tower,
 Resting now in the late sunshine,
But another day it must do brave work,
 On the day that is mine and thine.

Thou and I, by the belfry tower
 Stood at eve when the day was set.
Vows were made that were sweet to hear,
 —Sweet to make and forget.

" Some day, dear Heart, that bell shall sing
 One song and the same for thee and me,
When we pass through the church-yard gate
 With our goodly company."

The ringer is hired for the morrow by thee,
 And so he ring loud thou wilt feast him well,
Go, bid him make the bell sway long,
 It hath a strange tale to tell.

And start thou not from thy darling's side
   When I shall pass through the church-yard gate
Thy festal day shall be my festal day,
   And I too in state, though more solemn state.

And start thou not from thy darling's side
   When the bell rings on as they bear me by,
Saidst thou not it should ring for we twain,
   And our goodly company?

They shall not bear me 'twixt thee and thy bride,
   No more than thy vow do I seek of thee,
So that the bell shall sing that day
   One song and the same for thee and me.   .

SEPARATION.

If it were land, oh, weary feet could travel,
If it were sea, a ship might cleave the wave,
If it were Death, sad Love could look to heaven,
And see, through tears, the sunlight on the grave.
Not land, or sea, or death keep us apart,
But only thou, oh unforgiving Heart.

If it were land, through piercing thorns I 'd travel,
If it were sea, I 'd cross to thee, or die,
If it were Death, I 'd tear Life's veil asunder
That I might see thee with a clearer eye,
Ah, none of these could keep our souls apart.
Forget, forgive, oh unforgiving Heart !

FROM HIM TO HER.

"And now good morrow to our waking souls,
Which watch not one another out of fear."
—*John Donne.*

"AND is this all of love?" we cry
   With dreary eyes, and disenchanted
We turn a shuddering shoulder to
   The form that once our visions haunted.

Earth's saddest joy, its sweetest dole,
   In cloying flavors we have tasted,
The ghost of my clean, last year's soul,
   Bids me regret the hours I've wasted.

The bloom of Soul, Love's sacred mists,
   Reckless, we brushed aside forever.
Last night we loved; in gray To-day
   We both are very fain to sever.

Our plans to meet, our frenzied love,
  We view to-day with sad derision.
In this cold dawn your face seems changed
  From that which filled my dreams elysian.

And was it we who fiercely kissed,
  Our lips with rapture crushed together?
That was last night, to-day, my Dear,
  Has brought more chill and wintry weather.

Among the gods we lived last night
  In highest heaven, and now 't is over.
But I have lost my soul for this,
  While you—have only lost your lover,

BEREFT.

I let you go from me without a heart-break,
    For now at first, the old dream holds me fast.
Our lips have clung together, oh, so often !
    How can I feel this last kiss is the last ?

Go, then, grown weary of the old embraces,
    Nor think that you have left me quite forlorn.
I am contented to dwell henceforth in twilight,
    For once mine eyes have looked upon the morn.

A REMONSTRANCE.

NAY, mourn not so, my friend, not so,
　　Though once beloved, and now forsaken,
Though grief must go with you through life
　　And waken daily when you waken,
The dear, immortal Past is yours,
　　And will not leave you, or be taken.

Pity, instead, the poor like me,
　　Who own no golden Yesterday,
Whose roads have led through gloomy forest,
　　'Neath skies of chill and hopeless gray,
—Who cannot, in the time of Winter,
　　Look back and think, "It once was May!"

FOREWARNED.

I.

THE paths seem long that once were short for me,
  The ways that once were smooth, are hard and
    rough,
Old griefs and joys seem strangely near once more,
  My times for rest are never long enough.
The task undone may still unfinished lie,
And all my laughter breaks short in a sigh.

II.

Even so, some little leaves upon the trees,
  Withered in May, turned sere before their time,
Feel the strong breeze loosen their tender stems,
  To warn them they must go ere life's at prime,
To whisper, ere it drifts them all below :
"Leaves, little leaves ; make ready, you must go."

AN OLD BURDEN.

AND how is it when Love comes?
　　Tired feet shod with strength to run,
Bitternesses turned to sweets,
　　Shadows short in mid-day sun,
New cares risen, old cares ended,
　　Peace and passion strangely blended.

And how is it when Love goes?
　　We seek not what was before,
Teach our hearts some other tune,
　　And put by the look Love wore,
For since first the seasons ran,
　　Love comes only once to man!

ASSURANCE.

Would I, once dead, come back and haunt thee,
    Love ?
—Jealous of happy days that still were thine,
That thou couldst yet rejoice in warm sunshine,
And hatred stir thee, and hot passion move.

Would I, an icy breath, return to thee ?
    —To chill thy blood, and freeze thy heart with
        fear,
    To stand, a wraith, 'twixt thee and love's sweet
        cheer,
And make thee tremble with my voiceless plea.

Nay, Love, forget the green spot where I lie,
    And if too strong the wish to come to thee,
    No voice or spirit shalt thou hear or see,
Only across thy harp, one tender sigh.

HELIOTROPE.

THIS is the flower we loved, whose sultry scent
   Recalls the one sweet thing in all the world,—
      Delight,
Whose breath is love itself, who drinks the sun,
   And loves its fierceness more than dewy night.

This is the flower you killed, one August noon,
   Jealous because it laid upon my breast,
Jealous because it held the sacred place
   Where your tired head alone might dare to rest.

A PASTORAL.

O WOULD I were a blossom, then he would look
    upon me !
  He has a heart for fields and flowers, but none,
    alas, for me.
Or would I were a little wave, by wind and tide set
    moving,
  I would beat myself against his boat, as he sails
    out to sea.

O Love, be wise ; the blossoms will fade as soon
    as gathered,
  While set me in thy bosom, I will bloom for many
    a day.
And out upon the ocean the winter storms are
    raging,
  'T is safer far for thee to bide within love's land-
    locked bay.

THE JUNE STORM.

Two clouds, wind-hurled together,
Driven by the guilty weather
  Through darkness dense and warm.
Day into dusk was waning,
And in our breasts, past feigning,
We heard love's voice complaining,
  —The Spirit of the storm.

No thought of world withheld me,
All Nature's force compelled me
  To sink between your arms.
With yearning groans of thunder,
Heaven rent her veil asunder,
Showed lightnings hiding under,
  — Showed all her awful charms.

69

We, after kindred fashion,
Shared heaven's deep throes of passion,
  Its pangs of love and pain.
'T was sweet, beyond believing,
'T is past, beyond retrieving,
I hear, in my fierce grieving,
  Those beating tears of rain.

A DEPARTURE.

HOPE left me one black day,
Whither ?   Wherefore ?   Who can say !
  All I know is this :
One black day with strange surprise,
I saw pity in his eyes,
  I felt pity in his kiss.

Hope left without one parting glance,
Now others hear her tunes, perchance,
But never in my ears again,
She sings the old, bewitching strain.

A SOLILOQUY IN CHURCH.

Ah, Love, look down across thy flock at me.
Thou art not always thus, too blind to see !
For here I kneel, half down the crowded aisle,
And in mine eyes,—for thee alone,—a smile.
Look at me once, and memories, I will swear,
Shall make thee falter in thy measured prayer.
Ah well, thou dost not dream to find me here,
So from neglect I will absolve thee, Dear.
These worshippers, in clouds of incense sweet,
The breath of prayer has bowed, like bending
     wheat
Before the wind, and clearly I can see
The chancel and the altar, lastly, thee !
Is thy soul filled with heaven ? Ah, one night
How all the moonlight drenched us with its white,
My face was strained up, then, to meet thine own,
And now thine eyes are blank of love as stone,
And on thy shoulder all my gold hair fell,
As rare a covering as that chasuble.

Thy kisses drowned me ; now a meagre dole
With chill and hasty lips thou giv'st the stole.
God has a holy life as due from thee,
But no such fervor as thou gav'st to me !
Sometimes,—I know thee !—all thy soul rebels,
Weary of chants, and prayers, and solemn bells.
Across this life, like music over snow,
Echoes must drift, of old words, sweet and low,
Half inarticulate, made hard to hear,
Because thy mouth was close on mine, my Dear !
O if to-day I paused,—harassed by grief,
—Or needing counsel,—pleading for relief,
—Or any pretty lie I choose to make,
To speak with thee again, for old love's sake.
Words might not lead thee from the way divine,
But well I know,—if,—if,—my hand on thine,—
What devil tempts me ? Nay, I love too well
To lure thy white, if faltering soul, to hell.
Go sink thy thoughts in prayer and litany,
I dare not touch thee, Love ; go free of me.
Ah, is it over ? Yes, the chant is done,
And through the glowing window pours the sun,

Sets a prophetic aureole round his brow,
The promise of the After to the Now.
The organ moans no more, the singers cease,
And we, the faithful, now may go in peace.
And he has gone,—why should I longer stay
Who came to see him, not to praise or pray ?
And I, to-day, when once outside this door
Have left him utterly, forevermore,
For so I love him.   Later, he will stand
Crowned, with the saints, a palm within his hand,
Straight, who once bent beneath the scourging rod.
His soul a cup, filled to the brim with God.
Purged clean of earth, his pure, transfigured eyes
Will never search for me in Paradise.
For me, a sinner, just to see him there
Will make, I think, a Heaven of anywhere.
God will blot out, that he be clear of woe,
The memory of our tender loves below,
For else, nor peace, nor palm would quite suffice
Without me, to make bliss of Paradise !

SLEEPLESSNESS.

There is one spot beneath you, frosty stars,
    Where I, this bitter night, might make my nest.
Where is one place alone, in all the land,
    Where I might take my fill of peaceful rest.

O over dark and frozen miles to speed,
    To take the flesh where the soul pants to be !
And then to find—who knows ?—an empty place
    With last year's leaves, to make a bed for me !

A SONG OF LIFE.

Did I seek life ? Not so ; its weight was laid upon
    me,
And yet of my burden sore I may not set myself
    free.
Two love, and lo, at love's call, a hapless soul must
    wake ;
Like a slave it is called to the world, to bear life, for
    their love's sake.

Did I seek love ? Not so ; Love led me along by
    the hand.
Love beguiled me with songs and caresses, while
    I took no note of the land.
And lo, I stood in a quicksand, but Love had
    wings, and he fled.
Ah fool, for a mortal to venture where only a god
    may tread !

AN APRIL PLAINT.

YES, hope is over : Spring shall stir the mold
　Until the meadows shine in green once more,
And melt the ice around the inlet's mouth,
　Until the happy ripples kiss the shore.

But thou, when wast thou stirred by any prayer,
　Or moved by love, as is the Earth by Spring?
Cold voice, if I but once could hear thee melt,
　And motherly, to some tired baby sing,

—If I could see those eyes, that make my day,
　Shine through warm tears, as does the sun through
　　　shower,
And those proud lips that care for smiles alone,
　Quiver and droop through one unhappy hour—

Then I should hope, and dream that Winter's frost
　Was yielding to the witchery of Spring.
But I have waited now, so long, so long,
　—So vainly, for its first sweet bird to sing !

SONG.

OLD AGE, we shall be sorry friends, 't is my belief,
　For thou wilt burn my hair to ashen gray,
　And thou wilt steal love's dear delights away,
And leave me nothing in their place but grief.

God grant that memory's light at least remain,
　To bathe thy dreary waste of cheerless snow
　With radiance of an Alpine after-glow.
So I shall dream of youth, nor feel my pain. ·

HARVEST-TIDE FOR ONE.

WHEN all the land with corn was green,
   And all the air was hot with sun,
I used to lean from yonder pane,
   Rebuked for this or that undone,
To look across the glad, warm fields,
   " For there," I thought, " I soon shall glean."
With happy dreams of harvest-tide,
   When all the land was green with corn.

When all the harvest fields lay shorn,
   And stubble was, where corn grew fair,
For others was the harvest gain,
   For me—the empty fields stretched bare.
Only God knows how sad they were,
   Those cold brown lands, once green with corn,
But they were what was left for me,
   When all the harvest fields lay shorn.

THE WISH.

Come, let us spend an idle hour in wishing,
  Like happy children on a summer's day,
Feigning we never spent a past together,
  Nor know what farewells we shall have to say.

And I will wish this silver tide of moonlight,
  That shows your tender face, and upturned eyes,
Its weary lips, half parted in their languor,
  Too tired with kissing me, to speak replies.

—I wish this silver tide of summer moonlight,
  Were that strange flood of ancient fairy lore,
Wherein the hapless mortal rashly plunging, ·
  Was changed from flesh to stone, forevermore.

Through the long centuries we should still be
      sleeping,
  And Time could never touch your luring charms,
And I, past any chance of changing fortune,
  Should hold you, through the ages, in my arms.

Ah, Sweet, the days are past of elfin magic,
  And you must fade like any other flower,
And at the longest, I can only linger
  To keep you in my arms, one fleeting hour.

Ah, Sweet, forgive the reverie's bitter ending,
  What, has my foolish fancy made you weep ?
Nay, close instead those white and weary eyelids,
  And dream we love forever, in your sleep.

A FOREST EPISODE.

In my forest grew an oak,
King among the woodland folk.
Proudly rose his lofty head,
Mightily his boughs were spread.
Just a little breeze one day
Touched his leaves in wanton play,
Round him in a frolic ran,
That was how the storm began.

Just that little breeze awoke
Longing in the lusty oak.
All the leaves sighed ; "Come again !"
Nor was the amorous prayer in vain,
For the breeze, in one short hour
Came in conquering whirlwind's power,
And the heart of oak was riven,
With one flash of fire from heaven.

TWO SONGS OF SINGING.

I.

Sing to me once again, till I forget
That now we hate, and dream we love on yet.
Thy voice, if aught on earth, can wake regret,
Sing to me once again, till I forget.

Sing ; at thy voice the old dream shall arise.
Make me thy fool, feed me again with lies,
—For I was happier, ere I grew so wise,
Sing ; at thy voice the old dream shall arise.

II.

When first I heard thee sing, O my Beloved,
Thy voice, like wine, ran through my sleepy blood,
Woke soul and flesh in answer to its pleading,
And thrilled the unstirred depths of maiden-hood.

Listening, I wept, with strange, delicious anguish,
Nor knew it was a bitter prophecy,
A dim foreshadowing to my troubled spirit,
Of future tears, that I must shed for thee.

HEINRICH HEINE.

God said : " I will make a poet,"
- And a soul was sent below,
With the singer's wings of rapture,
   With the sufferer's weight of woe.

God laid on the eyes, the poet's
   Awful gift of second-sight,
On the restless, questioning spirit,
   All the blackness of the night.

On the body, pangs of torture,
   Hell's own pains and love's sharp sting,
Doubt you woe must dower the poet?
   Hush, draw close and hear him sing!

CONFESSION.

CURSE, if thou wilt ; yet perchance thy curse
　　Is that which holds me, when I would pray,
Gives me this dumb and frozen heart,
　　To carry about in my breast all day.

Ah, but the night, the night is thine,
　　Thou art avenged in the sinking night,
Sick unto death of an alien love
　　My soul is with thee from light to light.

His arms enfold me, persistent lips
　　Plead not in vain for an answering sign.
How should he dream that I feign the mouth
　　Seeking my own, is not his, but thine !

A RETROSPECTION.

THIS place is Paradise.   I grant you, dusk
Just melting into night, and swooning scent
Of dew-drowned roses, and the rich, dim fields
And half a mile away, the sea, that dreams
Upon the shore's white breast, and in its sleep
Whispers, are well for you.   For me, alas,
I crave a certain heated street to-night
Far down the city, mean and dull enough,
Its dingy, staring houses set a-row,
With windows open to the heavy air.
Among them, like the rest, save to my eyes,
To which it stands as clearly separate
As might a palace,—temple, rather say,
——A house that held what joy the gods ordained,
And set for my whole share in weary life.
And there 's a room, narrow, with four close walls,
A little place so consecrate to love,
It seems Queen Venus must be wroth with one
Who dares to step inside with clothen feet.

Dim ?   Ay, it was but litten scantily
With one small window,—dim as any shrine,
More glorified by love than sun or moon,
Yet was there light enough to show his eyes,
——Or was it they that made the gloom to glow ?
And in the tarnished mirror on the wall
To startle us, with shock of sudden sight
That repetition never dulled to us,
Of two dim faces, passion-pale, whose eyes
Made out the strange reflection, as a scroll
Writ backward, writ to read before a glass,
That never any other way reads plain and clear,
And learned, such times, what love had done
    with us.
Cheek pressed to cheek we looked and read
    therein,
Then turned from it, and sighed, stretched empty
    arms,
And found no tender speech in any tongue
Was sweet enough for what we fain would say.
So each dumb mouth sought each, in dearth of words,
And in that barren place Love stayed with us,

And in the silent hours he taught us all
His sacred mysteries, whereof we learned
With willing hearts, and drank with willing lips
Of every cup that Love's hand proffered us.
Would I might seek that little room to-night,
And pay to Love the debt I owe for this.
And pour a last oblation out to Love,
Who gave all joy to me.   It should be mete
For one who is so great and strong a god,
A crimson tide, but not of any wine,
Poured out most freely, with unfaltering hand.

IGNIS FATUUS.

THE pathway led through marshy land,
　My weary feet slipped in the ooze,
The drenching fog clung close around,
　Yet never did my will refuse
To travel on, to crush the rising moan,
Nor question why my way was set alone.

Across the marshes came the sound,
　Mist-muffled, of the lonely sea.
I passed the landmarks, one by one,
　This slimy stone, that rotting tree.
" Nearing the end," I told my fainting soul,
" Be brave ; we soon shall reach the journey's goal."

How could I know when night closed in,
　That ghastly light would haunt the moor ?
——To lead me back to whence I came,
　Always ahead, a Devil's lure.
So Hell gave them the race, and left for me,
The faint and mocking laughter of the sea.

LONGING.

Would God that I this day might take my rest
Within the quiet bounds of Paradise,
Where green the meadows spread for weary feet,
And peaceful looks the land to weary eyes.

Would God that I, in heaven's placid sea,
Might sink the dragging weight of memory,
The heavy burden of that vain regret,
That long as time shall last, must haunt me yet.

TIME'S REVENGE.

PARTED lips with victory sated,
  Dreaming head and outstretched form,
Now the face is pale with waking,
  That you once kissed crimson-warm.

O 't is Nature's just requital,
  You shall no more vigils keep.
I, who laughed to scorn your watching,
  Now am jealous of your sleep !

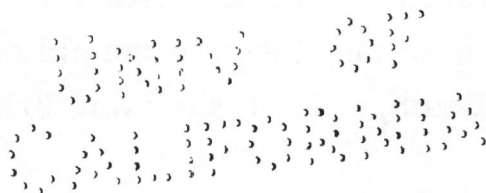

SOLACE.

In your arms but yesterday !
Where, to-morrow ?
Shuddering Sorrow
Gazes down, and sees the waiting clay,
Gazes up, and Heaven is far away,
Yet Flesh and Soul must go, though fain to stay.

.In your arms but yesterday !
—Softly sleeping.
Now, no weeping
Gains from Death, one little hour's delay !
Then hold me closer, in the old sweet way,
And Death, at least, shall find brave Love at bay !